TOO LATE TO BE A FORTUNE COOKIE WRITER

BY MARCY HEIDISH

A Woman Called Moses
a novel based on the life of Harriet Tubman

The Secret Annie Oakley
a novel based on the legendary sharpshooter

Witnesses
a novel based on the life of Anne Hutchinson

Miracles
a novel based on Mother Seton, first American Saint

Deadline
a novel of suspense

The Torching
a novel of supernatural suspense

A Dangerous Woman
Mother Jones, An Unsung American Heroine
a novel of a self-proclaimed Hell Raiser

Destined To Dance
a novel about Martha Graham

ALSO BY MARCY HEIDISH

Who Cares? Simple Ways YOU Can Reach Out

A Candle At Midnight

Soul And The City

Defiant Daughters: Christian Women of Conscience

TOO LATE TO BE A FORTUNE COOKIE WRITER

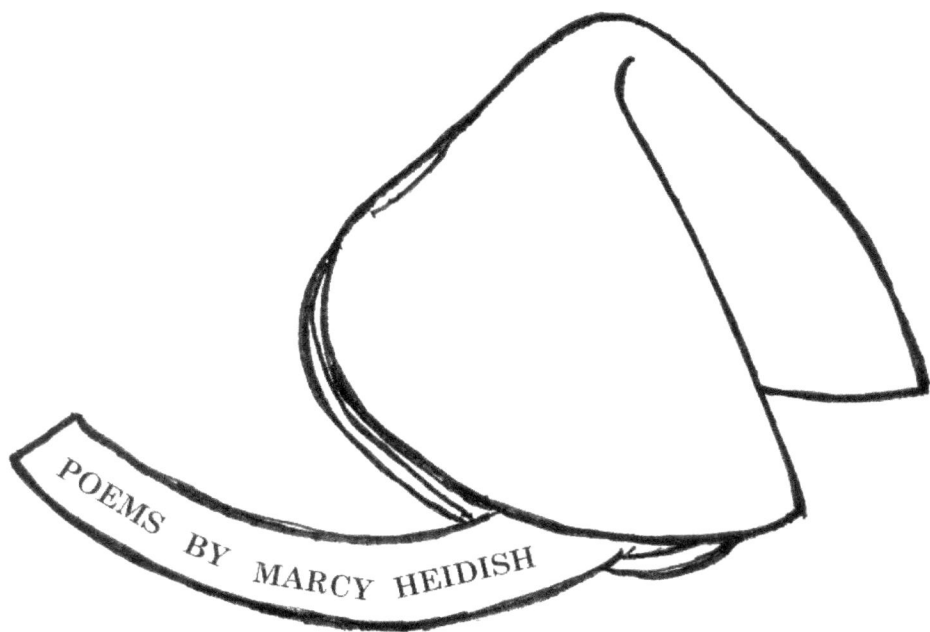

POEMS BY MARCY HEIDISH

Dolan & Associates, Publisher

TOO LATE TO BE A FORTUNE COOKIE WRITER

Copyright © 2013 by Marcy Heidish

LIBRARY OF CONGRESS CATALOGING-IN-PUBLICATION DATA
Heidish, Marcy.

p.cm.
ISBN: 978-0-9831164-8-6
Library of Congress Control Number: 2013951208

Cover: Design and Original Art by Marcy Heidish

Dolan & Associates, Publisher
Printed in the United States of America
....
First edition

FOR

CAROLINE LALIRE

IN LOVING MEMORY

~~~

And here face down beneath the sun
and here upon earth's noonward height
to feel the always coming on
the always rising of the night.
~~Archibald Macleish

Between my finger and my thumb
the squat pen rests.
I'll dig with it.
~~Seamus Heaney

What is closest to the heart comes out.
~~Irish proverb

CONTENTS

3. RIPENING

4. RAMBLING

6. REMEMBERING

1
Introduction

LATER

It's too late for me
to pull a full all-nighter
to be a deep sea diver
or a skilled bookbinder
or a fortune cookie writer

it's too late for me
to be an easy daughter
true to proffered maps
fulfilling all the shoulds
the woulds the coulds

it's too late for me
to right wrong turns
or mistaken choices
one composite Wrong
mine yours theirs ours

it's too late for me
to repeat confessions
and recycle my sins
I find absolution is
increasingly elusive

But wait:
it's not too late
to make one more run
and explore what's here
there is still some time
to probe the layered years

2
Running

GOING THE DISTANCE

a lifetime of running
is there a prize?

no one knows I ran for years
no one heard me slice the wind
no one saw me flash like glass
no one felt the air fly by
as I ran for my life

first I was running to flee
then I was running to find
now I'm tracking my runs
since the white finish line
jumped out of the dark
not yet imminent
but closer, closer

I now suspect
life is the Boston Marathon
with start times and end-lines
and in between
you just keep running
with euphoric highs
with serious strains
with second winds
and bottled water

of course there are
red lights and rest stops
weather curbs Velcro
these are the details
these are the detours
but not The Story
that is in the running

PILGRIMAGE

These old dirt roads
may thicken like honey
or fragment like salt
sprinkled by the sun

a simple walk, it seems,
the sky is a blue circus tent
its tough strings tethered
to a distant red lighthouse

each shaggy path is lined
with guardian junipers
ink-dark umbrellas in rain
and at noon but they know

what you soon will learn —
this walk never ends and
never remains simple
just when you're striding

a flat road spikes steeper
and sometimes you crawl
drinking the dust but
comrades rise beside you

to watch for pitfalls
dragons thieves even so
remember to sing as you go
and above all — tell stories

Stories alone pave the road.

UNEXPECTEDLY

This is how it works:

You hold still
you don't breathe
and the future
can't find you
and everything
will be the same.

I moved
I breathed
and the future
knew where
to find me
and nothing was
ever the same.

the future
I got was not
what I chose
at the big store
just in case
but another map
opened to me.

the planets
looked different
from this location
Venus, pin-sharp,
evading my one
grasping hand
my wide eyes.

The street where
I lived wasn't there
anymore but as
years swept by
the future could
always find me

unexpectedly.

NIGHT FLIGHTS

Consider now the possibilities:
If our souls could travel while we sleep,
in the guise of invisibility,
they could make a geographic sweep,

to pacify global insomniacs
to interrupt and intercept bad dreams
to distribute aphrodisiacs
or inspire new artistic themes.

Your spirit seeks spirituality?
Dispatch it to Tibet, maybe to Lourdes,
or send it to a new locality:
Fiji's islands or the Nordic fjords.

Required for such peregrinations:
all souls have a round-trip obligation.

HOW I LEARNED TO RUN

as a child I trained at home
always on my own
I didn't get the shoes
I didn't get the sweats
I didn't get the books

but I did run
my God I ran
I was a sprinter
they run on nerves
I ran on panic
is that different?

my track was through
our expansive home
a straight shot from
the bedroom wing
to the pantry kitchen
and the staff quarters

I could run it in the dark
I could run it in my sleep
I could run it backwards
I could run it on the ceiling
no choice here I had to run

down the long broad hall
past the sunny photographs
the brass bowl of peonies
the prized Picasso dove
peace caught in its beak

while at my back I heard
scorching voices steam
from the master suite
doors slam glasses smash
faster I ran faster then

dodging a console's edge
a floor lamp a chair leg
grab a wall swing around
watch that corner
escape the cross-fire

worse than that is
hostage-taking jerking me
this way that way no way
so it was I had to run
gasping loud grasping air

until I saw the pantry light
and I threw myself at it
hurtling toward refuge

ROMANY GRANDMOTHER

In a line of painted wagons you
were born. "On roads," you said,
"We lived, we died." A "Gypsy"
compania was your first tribe.
There you did and did not thrive.

At fourteen you ran into the dark,
leaving kin and that old man you
must wed — to Bucharest you fled
alone, never allowed to go home.

You sewed to pay your passage
sailing with scarves and an icon.
You, frail as forsythia, firm as fists,
took your icon through Ellis Island.

Old when I was young, you were
doll-like and diamond-hard
smelling of paprika and peaches
you sewed my father's "breeches."

Now I face aging and think of you;
I am ashamed to admit what's true:
You journeyed into the Unknown
and I fear traveling to God alone.

GOOD HUMOR

How those children ran to me—
I can see them still, years later:
small shadows like cut-outs
emerging from the warm dusk.

They came when they heard my call
as if I was some kind of Pied Piper
with jangling bells instead of a flute.
Bells or flutes — they didn't care.

Every summer evening in the 1950s,
it was the same thing: Twilight, running
feet, a stampede to my back door, then
sticky nickels and smooth cool ice cream.

Each child had a favorite. Boy, was I
in trouble when I ran out of these:
Almond Crunch, Chocolate Éclair, and
Strawberry Sundae frozen to a stick.

Everybody watched for me in those days
and I was one of 2,000 trucks at our peak.
The owners liked to say we were a fleet,
in our prime, an armada of chilled treats.

We slowed down in the Seventies as
those kids grew up and things were not
the same. The ice cream never changed —
only the kids and what made their dreams.

An old-timer now, I'm not what I once was.
The company displays me as a relic of our
golden years, when rock and roll came in
we went out, glad we couldn't see ahead.

I know what's next for me. I'll be on the
junk heap or sold for my working parts.
My engine is still pretty good — and
my rear suspension can't be beat, you bet.

Whoever comes along and looks
around the heap and buys my parts
will own a piece of twilight when
summer's children ran to me.

TINY BLUE CHAIR

I ran from you when the madness began
and your face wasn't yours anymore
and you yelled "Go to hell" on the street

yours was the face I had always wanted
to see in my mirror one day some day
when I wasn't eleven years old anymore

yours was a dense emerald gaze
like a medieval maze that drew me
in until I thought I'd found the center

no one else had an aunt who was Paris
and perfume — and that oddity, in 1958,
power with an office and a briefcase

you could hold fire in the quick flash of
your cigarette lighter and you drank
Scotch neat, like a man, I thought

in church I watched your etched profile
veiled by the tremulous membrane
of your lace mantilla and you smiled

you only wept on Good Friday when
we made the Stations together but
then you began weeping at mass

at street corners and cash registers
and near a gutter on Fifth Avenue
where you threw your wedding ring

frightened, I ran for help but I didn't
think help would be the hospital,
the psych ward with no way out

breakdowns haunted your family,
I overheard, but I couldn't see
why you went without goodbyes

I erased your face from my mirror then
afraid I might turn into you as I'd wished
but I did get one package from you:

a tiny beaded wire chair, turquoise blue,
made in group therapy, with a note:
"God's here — please pray anyway."

I never saw you again, despite requests
what you left to me is simple but strong
your faith and a miniature blue chair.

GOOD SAMARITANS

Don't we all run past that man in the ditch,
and try not to look, more often than not?
Even so we think of him, that's the hitch.
Who is he, anyway, a tramp or what?

No one has the time to rescue strangers
and if one does there are legal angles,
not to mention a fair chance of danger;
best pass on that complex little tangle.

Some do-gooder stops and reaches down
into the ditch. Maybe one of us should go?
But the fallen man could be a convict
or a terrorist, a thief, who knows?

At last, we decide to act, not hesitate,
but the ditch is empty; we're too late.

THE TROUBLE WITH MORNING

It runs at us too fast
shaking us awake
jolting our hazed brains
with alarming clocks

and forcing us from
the warm womb of bed
to the shock of rain
contained in a glass box

we are rushed through
our personal toilette
under the lidless glare
of voyeuristic lights

we must grab gulp
grapple with our food
while we taxi on the
day's crammed runway

then there is the traffic
the trudge the train
the push run nudge
to move faster still

if morning were gentle
it would be disgraced
today's dawn must
mime a racer's pace

FIVE A.M.

Cleansed
by submersion
in its nightly
bath of darkness
the tall tense city
stretches toward
the yawning dawn
as its grid-work
and its towers
glass steel stone
dress themselves
in shades of copper
deepening to bronze
while a young doctor
runs down the stairs
in a hospital to an
operating room
five high floors
above the city's
gleaming streets
where the surgeon
gowned and gloved
tells a nurse to
take a step back
before he straddles
the operating table
to wrest from a man's
throbbing stolid chest
an icepick

THE WOMEN'S SHELTER

Storms slam the city
and nine homeless women
run to this small shelter's
higher and drier ground.

Now the lights flicker,
sending come-and-go
shadows over figures,
drenched and pungent,
crowded into what we
dare to call "the lounge."

In that dim room I see
a mass of female bodies
bundled in soaked cloth,
bound together as if one,
a mound with nine faces,
creased as pillowcases.

Now I recognize them,
different as fingerprints:
Jane has a purple hood
and Gig tracks the stars;
Jo brings bits of boxwood.

Nan recites all the psalms;
Lil's one china cup, her own,
reminds her of a lost home.
Nell avoids all barking dogs
and Jenny has a silver comb.

We talk and proffer blankets
but the women's feet are wet.
Worn sneakers are shed so
towels can replace each pair
and I kneel, untying laces.

Sneakers, wrapped in foil,
like long baked potatoes,
go into the stove to broil
or bake in lumpish rows;
there's no time to recoil.

"I've got hot feet," Jo crows,
pulling on her running shoes.
We fill the stove once again
and take pride in our results.
Small wins here are big news.

A FRIEND'S DEPARTURE

"The centuries have not been kind to frescoes, fading them to faint
ghosts of themselves...." The New York Times, October 20, 2008

Finally the stucco crumbles
as the painted walls collapse

but early on signs appear
thready cracks then colors

the blue pigment changes first,
fading from cerulean to gray

the gilded haloes last longer
— metal survives watercolor

outlines fade leaving frescoed
figures suspended in the air

disconnected from each other
and the world they once knew

you are fading like a fresco
paling but remaining near

as your silent cancer waits
to steal your life from us

your blue robe has gone gray
the gold surrounding you will stay

INVENTORIES

Houses crowd my past
like chairs strewn on a
spare November beach.

I've left ten roofs, two hearths,
twelve beds, four patios,
and seven states, East to West.

A pilgrimage, perhaps? Or my
last try at finding Oz? Now I can
claim many roots — and none.

All merge into a single voice, a rich
contralto, and this, in turn, blends
like distant music into distant skies.

Now my home is a tin archangel,
hammered to a simple board,
long-time guardian and friend,

and the figure of a bird, hand-carved
twenty years ago from a hefty gourd;
books, Breviary, one wooden desk;

one Mexican candlestick, one stone
Celtic Cross and one dark green
glass Shamrock — made in China.

All the rest has blended with the wind.

RECOGNITION

Regrets, those uninvited guests, arrive
for longer stays than many hosts expect
and if one should venture to contrive
exemption from regret he is suspect.

But which of us can blame such hosts?
Do we fail to see ourselves among them?
We would rather paint ourselves as ghosts
in a tableaux of shamed women and men.

Denial is the drug of choice for pain
and pain companions genuine regret
but age gives us the wisdom to reclaim
our human frality, however imperfect.

Wisdom lacks glamor but it does live on
chanting within us like an antiphon.

3
Ripening

EROSION

Tell me once again
that I remain myself
though time is changing
me, crease by crease,
as evening takes a
living tree, branch by
branch, into invisibility.

Snows have sculpted
canyons of stone spires,
elegant, ecclesiastical,
while others have eroded.
A rock gets millennia,
a butterfly, one month,
and we — who can say?

In the glass today I saw
my grandmother, tall as
a tiger lily; she laughed.
Her eyes mine then gone.
She never saw a canyon;
darning her son's socks
taught her about erosion

She knew, as do the rocks,
erosion's not the enemy. It
is I, resistant to life's cycles,
who erodes what joy is left.
So tell me I remain myself,
even creased, and grandma
laughed, forty years deceased.

EARLY LOVE

The sun is a peach, half-ripened, at hand,
in the early hours of marriage.
When life is seen through a wedding band,
nothing within its scope is disparaged.

A first home's décor is thrift store wicker;
the first Christmas is a shared candy bar,
but films of this era will never flicker;
the outlines may fade, the content endures.

Love's opening flush cannot be replaced,
no matter what may occur at high noon,
and lovers will always feel the sun's grace
even if night steals its power too soon.

A marriage, like morning, may not be saved
but its early light stays with you to the grave.

LATER LOVE

Later love is like a windfall apple
good to last the winter in a cellar,
slightly dented and partially dappled,
still firm as a seasoned orchard-dweller.

This is fibrous love: tough, not sugary.
Its fruited heft will travel far and long,
as ally, never as adversary,
disinterested in collecting wrongs.

Older love keeps bedside vigils
but retains a knack for celebrating,
and in it gallantry resides until
the fruit offers itself up for baking.

Common but not commonplace this globe
encloses life's core and seeks nothing more.

IF

all our married days
pass before me now
and pause as if they
await my last review
one definitive and
clear command for
them to stay or go

on a hard marble sky
each day is etched
one after another
unchangeable but
visible and vivid
as I watch their colors
butter blood and brandy

I see you at the vineyards
of Chianti, an afternoon
embracing us with life
and I will take that day
along with me if I die
tomorrow during surgery

now the restless line
before me stirs and shifts
weary of its wait
and finally I call out
one word and only one
for all our days — "Stay!"

GOING UNDER

my arms are positioned
as if I might fly
but this body of mine
forms a Cross

I am told to start counting
backwards from ten
but even my cells
tighten up

"Relax," I am urged
in this frigid place
with its uncaring
hot lidless eyes

are they kidding or what?
No laughter here —
just a stark gaze —
I would guess not

"Maybe next year?"
I want to ask
but I am unable
to speak one word

again the surgical nurse
tells me to count
but the Lord's Prayer
is what she heard

I give in and count back
from ten to nine to...
a slide downward
into the dark

where all my yesterdays
wait to draw me
fathoms deeper
toward the past

and shared history
as centuries bleed
into each other and
carry me below

to the warm womb
where we rejoin
roots of our roots
of our roots

KEEPING TIME AT SIXTY

Sun on windy water
gulls sweep past
my wide-eyed
windows
to a new house

sun on its raw roof
half-finished
splinters lit by this
half-finished
morning

How many
mornings wait
to swing open
before me like
my kitchen door?

How many gulls
will I watch as
they arrow through
the corridor of air
beside my porch?

Mornings gulls
summers houses
no longer infinite
as they seemed when
I was twenty-four.

My grandmother often
dreamed of numbers
for a local lottery and
my father swore she
always won the purse.

If she dreamed the
number of her years,
she never said but
lived them and served
each to her family.

LOST & FOUND

The prodigal son finally returns
bringing home his issues and his laundry
and our settled lives begin to churn
as we sense the onset of a quandary.

When the lost are found do we forgive them
or resent them? Their reflection of us
could reveal a tramp or a tragedienne;
distance seems a better course than trust.

But wait! In an ancient tale we witness
a father's tenacious and tender embrace,
overwhelming his son with forgiveness:
a child who crawled his way back in disgrace.

Mercy unites us in age or in youth,
defying logic but defining truth.

SPEED

Faster now
life's grainy grit
sifts through
the stained strainer
in her hand.

Faster now
life's pensive paint
dries on
the swift fingers
of her hand.

Faster now
life's tidy ticks
grab all
the soft pauses
from her hand.

Sooner now
come the birthdays
come the wakes
crazy daze of dates
too jumbly to name.

Sooner now
comes the thinning:
hair, bones, skin
crazy maze of doctors
too many to blame.

Sooner now
comes the gaining:
weight, awe, grace,
crazy haze of wonder
too sacred to claim.

HEIGHTS

A thousand exclamation marks in green
jump up from the earth and join the jolt
of yolk-yellow things: crocus and daffodils
are the first to see — and to be seen.

All this from maligned and muddy ground
where, the child was told, we hide the dead.
Below, she heard, lies their invisible domain,
but the child has insights more profound:

Life surges from earth's fertile heft.
Death lurks *above* and not *below,* as
we believed; the child was not deceived.
Death stalks the heights but not the depths.

Above, nothing grows. Missiles streak,
lightning scalds. Heights, like pride, can
lead to falls and falls to death, this child
knows and she is well-qualified to speak.

When her mother holds the girl's head
out the window, sixteen stories up, and
city traffic screams below, and mother
threatens to let go, height equals death.

Life returns with a rescue and tears.
Though this child can't recall which of
her misdeeds prompted that penance,
heights will always prompt her fears.

Later, aging, she yearns to see
one detail she viewed as a girl:
grass growing from the tower of
an old cathedral's masonry.

Will she go? None can tell
who will rally and rebel and
wrench one final stream of
exclamation marks in green.

IN CHIANTI

We drink it as we watch it grow:
wine, red as plasma, shimmers
in the glass, and before us lies
its ancient source, green as
sage and jade, the vineyards,
spreading out of time and sight.

The slanting sun suddenly
illuminates our table, flash-
cube bright; the waiter kneels
to pour a circle of golden oil
and inky vinegar at its center:
a flower seems to fill the plate.

Later, as our headlights slash the
dark, I think of pasta marinara ---
and abruptly, Ella Stark. Homeless,
roaming an American city, she was
murdered in an alley. Ella is the
dark splash in that disk of oil.

Why now, why here? Why in Tuscany
does Ella Stark appear? Continents
and years away, on the verdant curve
of a rare day, we are near to her as
this evening's espresso. I can hear
her voice the last time we had talked.

Once, Ella said, she had a night
never quite forgotten. She was eating
chocolates as she read in her own bed
and knew, she said, that was about
as close to heaven as a person gets —
and I could count on that, she added.

Wine or chocolate — in the end, there
is little difference; God has countless
conduits and who am I to class them?
Perhaps Ella came to share our joy or
perhaps to warn us: *Remember! This
night isn't the end of the whole story.*

A JESUIT FATHER

Droll and small, a parish priest
stopped me after mass to say,
"This time don't just slip away."
He winked. "I am not a beast."

Knowing his name, I gave mine,
and he asked me to the rectory
the next day for Earl Grey tea.
"No agenda," he said. "Nine?"

"Nine," I wrote on a pad I saved.
So it began, on a Saturday, I think,
our long friendship passing in a blink,
lasting far beyond his narrow grave.

We grew close as parent and child;
His fatherhood a kind I never knew.
When he was sixty I was twenty-two
but we had no gaps to be exiled.

His Irish father labored in mills
and fell asleep still on his knees,
fingers tangled in Rosary beads:
a life fueled by prayer and will.

From immigrants this son emerged
a Jesuit, twelve years in formation,
always urged to take a good vacation.
Overworking, he refused to splurge.

As Novice Master he earned praise
but for him less was always more.
When a parish opened its oak doors,
he knew he had found his place.

This shrub of a man possessed
an ancient redwood's soul,
even though his trenchant jokes
could nip as thorns prick flesh.

He found weddings overdone:
"The performing arts," he sighed.
Fundraisers? "Combat duty," he
would grin, then grimace.

His dark eyes always filled
for the "Our Father" at mass.
His preaching, unsurpassed,
was to him merely "a frill."

Sudden strokes ended these.
He died in the Jesuit Infirmary
as he watched a documentary;
half-asleep, he left with ease.

His funeral would have fit
the wry term, "performing arts,"
but everyone wanted a part
in honoring his life's gift.

I watched his brothers set him
in the loamy summer ground.
Birdsong was the only sound
After the prayers dimmed.

"This time don't just slip away...:"
I recalled his first words to me.
Please rewind the tape I see.
Now I would command him to stay.

In Georgetown, I visit his grave
and ask him to abide with me.
He is not here, whisper the trees.
Without him it is harder to be brave.

THE POTTER

Traveling by train, she sees
the image of her wheel, a
spinning bowl of fire, on
the rain-wet window pane.

She wants to plunge
her fingers into grout-rich clay
and invent new planets in the
guise of pots and bowls —

all the globe-like shapes
she now creates, freed
at last to conjure them from
the understanding earth.

Once she painted grids,
sharp-edged rectangles
on unyielding boards —
unemotional best-sellers.

The juiced spray of an orange,
offered as a gift and sectioned
for her by a ninety-year-old
friend with trembling hands,

changed the artist in a day:
Was it the fruit's round form
or was it those arthritic hands?
She was not entirely sure.

Now the potter goes by train
to visit her friend and muse —
the magician in her life.

As a gift the artist brings
one round summer peach
and a sharpened knife.

MISS WITCHITA

I'll never be Miss Wichita again
I'll never be Miss Tennessee.
I'm too old for pageants anymore
now I'm pushing twenty-three.

I'll never hang another load
of wash but that's a big fat lie
I'll walk these clotheslines,
pins in hand, until the day I die.

I'll never get a washer-drier
wasted money, Billy says
since there's lines and sun
and I quit singing in the choir.

I'll never have a hair shop like
I wanted when Billy re-upped.
On this army post I'm just "wife;"
I wanted a different kind of life.

I'll never quit this wanting more
and sometimes I see myself on
the sea in a blue boat and me
the sails, strange as that seems.

I'll never stop seeing this even
after the dream falls to pieces
like an egg hit by a fork and I
wake, thinking I am fifty-three.

I'll never have a thing but fog
inside my house, hard to see
where things are so we move
around each other carefully.

I'll never quit chewing gum;
Billy won't quit his tobacco.
We'll be just the way we are
twenty years from right now.

I'll never know why one friend
saw great things in me. She
was a college girl but no snob.
We talked, both of us lonely.

I'll never be a college girl like
her or the wife of a draftee —
no way out for me. She said
I could be what I decide to be.

I'll never think she was right.
What was it in me she saw?
She couldn't grasp my dreams.
She's never been Miss Wichita.

CELEBRATION

A slender branch of chance
bends her way

this raw January day
when she hears

her tests are back and
all of them are "clear."

That word is a lamp hung
from the fingers of a tree

light on milk-slick snow
her face arms legs torso

until she is the lamp
the light the snow

DREAMING

In sleep I see:

a platinum lake
one small boat
berry-blue
two long oars
a young couple

the smile of their silence
comes over the water
they hug the shore
then each other

the boat overturns
but two heads bob
wet hair held hands
sparkling voices
crackle of laughter

and I awaken
wishing myself
into that boat
whether it's righted
or not

THE WHITE QUEEN

Winter is older than
her sibling seasons;
wiser and leaner,
ancient and able,
she's sharper, keener,
this white queen,
the great transformer.

Dame Winter alone
can catch fire in ice,
seal the earth in pearl,
change lakes into land
and the land into cream
and the rain into stars:
unique, no two the same.

The queen teaches us
strength with a cold wind,
then bestows a thaw or
sets trees to glimmering,
and as she chills she
also charms, guarding
the earth crust's harm.

She shows us how to
wait and how to turn
into a subtle sorceress,
but asks us to see in
her our own reflections.
We are her children if
we look into her mirror.

4
Rambling

A TASTE OF TURF

*D*on't eat dirt in Central Park."
At play there, we were warned
with ominous intensity
after one child was discovered
nibbling topsoil and bark.

City children all, we'd hoped
for his detailed report
but the grownups dropped a tent
of silence over this event
and the culprit, scolded, moped.

This did not make any sense.
Pilgrims kissed the ground
so why not taste it? Earth was
honored, lasting, vast, and
even older than our parents.

Why should we downgrade earth
with words like "dirt?" *Terra
Firma* was not mud to wash away,
nor was it cement or clay;
Earth had a distinctive worth.

Later, I saw immigrants press
their lips to a new land and I
recalled my childhood friend,
crouching underneath an oak,
tasting turf — New York's best.

Beyond curiosity — his spark —
did that boy sense some vitality,
land-locked, in what he saw,
enough to prompt a mortal's sin:
Eating dirt in Central Park?

ONE WORD

A man is kissing a loaf of fresh bread
as he waltzes alone throughout the night,
sailing about the guest room's narrow bed;
he sings one word to the yellow lamplight.

In five languages he carols, "Thanks,"
wishing he could be more transatlantic:
Grazie and *Merci*, *Tapadh* and *Danke*,
all sung as if each word were romantic.

In the safe house of a welcoming friend,
this hard man croons gratitude to the night.
His prison sentence has crawled to an end
this fresh bread is freedom he can bite.

What once he ignored he wishes to bless:
this long loaf of new life, yeasty with "Yes!"

EVENING VISITOR

Stars laser-bright
platinum the moon
air so tightly tuned
I could hear a voice
it seemed
anywhere in Santa Fe

the painting on my wall
hung that afternoon
sent a tribe of Sioux
riding through my
dining room

I left one long row
of votive candles to
make the riders glow.
watching them I knew
abruptly I was not alone

unseen, this visitor,
but a palpable guest
with a leathery essence,
yet I sensed no danger
as it seemed to view
the painting

the candle flames bowed
then rose up again
as if someone passed,
someone of honor,
and I sat believing

when you came in
to see the candles.
"I thought they'd burnt out,"
you said, distressed.
I stared at my sandals
lacking easy explanations

DON'T DO LUNCH

Let's cancel noon today.
Let's rethink the concept
for a moment anyway.

Let's recall the ancient view:
Demons stalk us at midday,
not at midnight, as we say.
Danger hides in front of you.

Think about the glare of noon,
The silent birds, the sleeping bees —
something in that sudden
stillness brings us to our knees.

Fill that gap! Ink me in! Have
a power lunch or two martinis,
but what's happening in Rome,
Madrid, or on Santorini?

Their residents close their shops
— noon is not the time for a fiesta —
and resolve that midday gap
with a sensible two-hour siesta.

This outwits the "noontide devils"
who play on our doubts and fears,
inducing despair, as demons can,
on the job thousands of years.

Evil presents few novel deceptions
but recycles Honorable Mentions.
If we cancel noon, teatime may be
next in line for demonic intervention.

BEACH ON SANTORINI

Early evening light
sets off two full nets
of sea-slick fish
swinging from the
hardened shoulders
of six strong men
trudging up the beach
leaning as into a wind

toward a lantern and
a bench bright with
well-honed blades
ready for the day's
last haul to spread,
silvery and alive,
across the plank
and surrender
to the knives.

Now the men are
only silhouettes
lithe as dancers
tending to the fish
and to their nets
in that silent smelly
work done with the
precision of a Mass.

Through this ancient
ritual spill thousands
of years, meals, nets,
fish, generations and
here time is absent,
irrelevant,
one endless
rope of human life.

CLIMBING IN CORTONA

As strangers
we meet
on the steep and sloping
street
climbing wordlessly
breathing as one
she with her cane
I with my boots
we lean into
the hill town
of Cortona.

Its narrow streets
like hallways
through a castle on a hill
winding upward
under a blue bowl of sky
lead us on until

we slow our pace as
she bends her head
a corolla of snow
and smiles at me
the stranger
the American
struggling to
keep up with her.

She waits for me
this woman in black
maybe eighty
I the novice
at fifty and we
go on together
as the ancient town
draws us higher.

How many women
have climbed this
street with canes
market baskets
laundry garlic
and Rosaries?

I am with them and
they welcome me
an endless line
of women
climbing through
the years
the centuries.

HOTEL IN FLORENCE

The bathtub alone
made me want to flee:

that long stretch of marble
like a queen's sarcophagus,
fitted with vermeil faucets and
centered in a room the size
of a four-car garage.

Was I lost in the Ufizzi
Museum or perhaps the home
of a modern Medici? I
guessed the hotel had erred
when giving this room to me.

The suite's expansive bed,
draped in pearly brocade,
lay amid frescoed walls
where Renaissance nobles,
laughing, played lutes.

I called the front desk only
to hear, Yes! This is my
my room for tonight. But
how to sleep here with all
those courtiers watching?

What is she doing in here? I
thought they murmured in
horror. *Ah... cosi e la vita!*
A maid came to turn down
the bed and run the bath.

From the regal sarcophagus,
I saw the frescoed ceiling and
tried not to let myself drown.
The nobles were looking on.

All night I saw the whites of
their eyes in the dimness and,
come dawn, they remained,
watching, winking, waiting.

Dating back over 20,000 years or more, the most ancient pictorial art was discovered in caves in southwest Europe.

THE CAVE

Always it starts
in the dark
and so it was
beyond memory.

I lift my oil lamp
as I enter the cave
and move down
a long and narrow
passage black as
dreamless sleep.

The dark admits me
as it did my father's
father's father bearing
the colors we mix —
reds yellows blues —
made by memory
and washed in place
with our moss mats.

far above my head
my people hunt
my children run
my wife stirs soup
but my hunt is here
where I seek the
horse within a horse
and he joins others

where there was
a wall of rock now
there are bison
there are ibex
there is what
never was before
rippling in my light

did you ever grip
a chunk of raw color
in your hand and
turn it into a deer?
Then you, distant
from me in time,
should not doubt
the magic here.

County Offaly, Ireland

THE BOG

This is where the earth
is stitched to sky. This
is where the world begins
and ends. This is where
a poet found his life and
where he chose to die.

Take the low road from
town as the day fades
and tawny light, long and
late, slants across that
sweep of peat wide open
to the sky. Go and wait.
Something will happen.
A bog reveals itself in
its own time and pace.

Once a lake-bed, then
a marsh, building for a
thousand and one years,
a bog is ugly/beautiful
floored feet deep with
dried moss we call turf.
Mind how you go. Mires
quake near scraps of
silvery water scattered
through brown peat.

Watch for workmen who
cut turf for fuel, light, heat;
men who know the way
to walk a bog and where
to set their feet. Corpses,
long preserved, lie below.
The turf's tannins keep
them so and stain the
diggers hardened hands.

The men skirt the white
lace of bog-lilies and the
grassy clumps of sedge.
Overhead herons wheel
and when the workers go
the bog spreads out alone:
Empty, full, raw and rich,
unimpressed by time.

IRISH ROADSIDE MADONNA

Her hands are fingerless
but they spread outward
mittened in cold limestone.
From one, like a kite's
string caught in a tree,
hangs a crystal Rosary.

Worn away by centuries
of pilgrims' lips
the Madonna's fingers
still erode and there
we can glimpse
faith in action
on stoic solidity.

The Madonna's
hem recedes
shaped by rain and touch
numberless the pleas
spoken and unspoken
by pilgrims who
also recede.

We leave remnants of
ourselves at these stone hems:
a note, a rose, a ring, a cross,
a row of small red vigil lights —
the shrines accept them all.

Here is what we always knew:
Holy ground is where we find it
and we mark that place
as a citadel against our fears
as a catchment for our tears
as a cradle for our years.

LEAVING IRELAND

W̲e could not stop its
coming, our last day
in Ireland, in Kilcree.

Too soon the darkness
drained away like ink
poured into earth and
the sky turned the color
of our father's eyes.

And soon the sunrise
melting like butter over
fields and rock walls,
stone laid on stone by
hands long gone to dust.

Beyond, the pastures'
blue-green haze where
cows appeared to float
as if at sea and grasses
sparked with flowers,
reds hot as embers,
yellows like cat's eyes.

Out with us then, our
packing yet undone,
to have a wander in
the wet glitter of grass
and didn't we beg each
each branch and bush
to wait for us, to will us,
woo us back to Kilcree?

VAIL, COLORADO

mountains
grip the sky's
wide hem
like giants
vying for
attention
and sun
is a gold
button on
a cloak
of thin
blue air
until fluid
shadows'
waves rise
to melt the
mountains
into night
darkness
hides the
glimmering
gold clasp
of the new
day's cape

SAILS

That afternoon in Maine comes back in parking lots,
on line in pharmacies and supermarkets' aisles
where metal carts collide and clash and clang...

...and fade into the song of buoys bobbing in
green water near a rocky coastline's harbor on a
blue-sky July day, one-hundred years ago, it seems,

sailing on the jib we navigate our way to a mooring
and once ashore, find a friend's house and a dock,
its wood sun-warmed, where we share simple fare:

fresh lobster with melted butter and tart lemonade:
nothing new for us but new it tastes, just invented,
and just below us the green water is whispering

secrets known since the first tides, before time was
before there were words and names for white mist,
and we thought but did not say: *I'll remember this*.

Before dusk, we sailed on a starboard tack toward
an ember of red sun and I hear the snap of sails,
the tug of tide, as I stride a supermarket's aisle.

SO?

The great cathedral arches its long
spine over its soaring space and
again I find myself at my center;
no ticket needed to enter.

On my knees in a lake of blue light,
I sense a presence hovering nearby,
pacing with a charge of urgency.
What is it? A spiritual emergency?

Alarmed, I rise from the small kneeler
and turn toward the pacing woman,
young, tense, blonde, chewing gum
She doesn't kneel; she stares at me.

"So?" She says. "Who does your hair?"
I am speechless as she presses me.
"So who?" She repeats. "Give, share."
"What?" Startled, I swear. "God—"

Maybe I heard wrong — I stammer.
"Sure." She snaps as if I've damned her.
Too late I understand her sarcastic air.
She thought I claimed God does my hair.

I can't find her and I can't right my wrong
but I'm oddly grateful she is in this throng.
Sacred space holds unnumbered seekers,
or a cathedral would only be bleachers.

GRATER, NEW YORK

He squats, grating beets,
on a swatch of sidewalk
in midtown Manhattan
where he sells his tools
from a blue yoga mat.

Crowds step over this
unshaven man with his
array of raw vegetables.
"Buy from me," he calls.
"I'm a trained mechanic."
Tattooed teens scan his
carrots as they demand:
"Is this stuff organic?"

A jostling clan shoves
the peddler away from
a decorative fountain
where they take a drink.
When a cyclist, in skirts,
skims the grater, he yells:
"This is my damn work."
The cyclist yells, "Jerk!"

A blondish dog-walker
on a cell phone tramples
the beet-grater's set-up.
"You pay," he shouts;
the dogs pull her away.
The beet-grater, cursing,
packs up tools and mat,
then, skyward, hurls
his prized carrot curls.

No one sees him leave.
The beet-grater is done,
or so it seems, but his
will is not diminished.
Relocating, he starts up
a new gig, JUST FRUIT.
If that's not successful,
he'll go back to pretzels.

THAT OTHER PLACE

a house bearded in ash
dust abruptly silver-
struck by fingers
of fading sun
gapped floorboards
dropping shafts
attic to cellar
half-hinged doors
hanging at a slant
window panes
a webbed maze
of cracks and
crazed patterns
like hoarfrost
walls with squares
of nothingness
where photos hung
the crooked gate
a kitchen plate
left on the steps
for a lost cat
and wind in
the chimney
always keening
sighing saying
"Here I lived
when I survived
depression."

ON RETREAT

Silence,
tentative as twilight,
tangible as toast,
comes over us
as we wander the
monastery's land.

The grounds spread
out around us now:
Fields minted
green with white
lilies: ballerinas
caught *en pointe*.

We stroll or settle
at a niche, a rock,
a bench. We avert
our eyes from a dead
tree, lightening-
struck and black.

Instead we watch
the chapel's spire,
a needle threaded
with morning light.
We are free to pray,
journal – levitate?

Still, that dead tree
disturbs me. I turn
away and scan the
words given to us
for our own reflection.
Jolted by them, I wince.

"*In the midst of life
we are in death.*"
Why this antiphon?
I came here to find
simple serenity on
this Ash Wednesday.
.

I contemplate the
black tree and the
verse before me;
now I begin to see.
True serenity doesn't
equal simplicity.

5
Reclaiming

WOMAN-TREE

Fierce and focused as a warrior's gaze,
searing as the bluest core of a flame,
is the passionate love for a child raised
as your own marrow, member, membrane.

Ferocious is the love that child returns,
finding one home in one figure, one face.
I am such a child whose loving has burned,
not with mere gratitude, but sheer grace.

More mother than mother, you are the tree
to whom I am grafted, branches and leaves,
nor could Death ever remove you from me;
in my own greening you live as I grieve.

She who does not tear the baby in two
is truly the one who is mother to you.

NORA

Your voice, grainy and low,
its Irish lilt like metered verse,
forms my earliest memory.
I rode a sonnet into life.

Your voice and your scent,
vanilla, mint, cigarettes,
sealed me like an envelope
as I rode on your arm or hip.

Your voice and your eyes,
two blue sparks from tinder
and that untamed red hair
I rode with it in my mouth

Your voice telling stories by
the hundred: rebels and saints,
pirates, and poets and queens:
I rode with you to their worlds

Your voice got you the job:
you talked your way in —
a lone immigrant country girl,
running a doctor's household.

Your voice ordered a fine home,
a Manhattan penthouse, with
its warring family; there china
smashed but you were unfazed.

Your voice and your room behind
the kitchen were home to me; safe
from nightly parental warfare —
you talked me to sleep in your bed.

Your voice was not your sole power:
people made way for you on streets;
shopkeepers rushed your orders and
doormen nodded to you — but why?

Your voice — it was more than that.
you were a primal force like a wind:
a country's teacher's daughter
quoting Yeats as you pared potatoes.

WHAT COUNTS?

Fireflies cut button-holes
of light into the dark
serge of a summer sky.

Rising from tall grasses
others nick the night and
fly, flit, flicker, die.

How can this be done
so casually? I turn to
find out what you see.

I suspect you learned
this choreography
from the fireflies.

I'm young, you're antique
(thirty-five), and you know
what seems to me oblique.

You taught me that word
and now it comes to mind
as a new thought occurs.

In my nine Julys, we've
seen generations and
ancestors of fireflies.

"Why can't they last?"
I demand. Your quirky
answers always satisfy

and so I wonder why
you pause, hesitating
to measure your reply.

"Listen now." Your blue
gaze burns. "What matters
is the flying, not the dying."

I kick our porch seats
three times and, silently,
ashamed, I start to weep.

"Why should they die?"
Your answer, a surprise:
"Why should they fly?"

THE PEAR

When she halved a ripened pear
it opened for her like a book
with pages of pale pulp and
the smell of summer there.

Nora knew she could not turn
this immaculate fruit into a frill
served on a plate but it was late;
the guests were expecting dessert.

Her employer's party had to wait
as she tried to save the pear and
its kindred, as tender and fair.
She combed the pantry for cake.

Finding none and sensing doom
she made her sacrifice and served
the cloven pears, excepting one ---
this she spirited off to her room.

In her work she tended things so fine
she trembled as she polished them.
After life changed and she got this job,
"Nothing fine," she said, "Was mine..."

Except this pear, and in the dark
she memorized its curved torso shape.
Then, before the fruit started to decay
she buried her pear in Central Park.

HOLY SMOKE

I prayed with fire as a child
lighting vigil candles with you
in every church we knew
where our murmured pleas
dipped and danced for God
even after we were gone.

In those naves' dim caverns
the same scent prevailed:
flowers, incense, floor wax,
mingling with spent matches
and some of them were mine.
There I learned silent prayer.

Its power did not snap after
we saw a homeless woman
pilfering the Poor Box and
a drunk asleep in a back pew.
We lit candles for those two;
You said, "That we must do."

Grown, I light candles alone,
but not alone, as the flames
dance on for those unknown
who stand with me. "How?"
A friend asks. I tell her what
you told me: "It's a mystery."

SPUDS

Nora pares them into
a blue moon of a bowl
as I sit by her knees

where I receive her gift:
a bog-brown bracelet
one long spiraled peel

from this lumpish tuber
ancient food of the Irish
and now food for us.

Sealed in rare safety
I descend with Nora
down below the ground

through our pantry drawer
that deep black space
cool as a cellar or a grave

within this covert place
potatoes await their time
to rise up into the light

until then they give off
the scent of night that
draws us into the earth

"There are hidden births,"
she tells me to show
how the dark can grow

in humble guise, the Bread
of Life, sacred to the poor
who dig this gift, this gold

LIGHT FLOOD

It's Nora with her flashlight
who finds me under the bed
afraid of the darkness
after the hall lamp burned out

It is she who takes me through
the house with that lit torch
to show all is clear
in the corners I doubt

It is she who wakes me early
to watch daylight's shy return
as she predicted
giving most of my fears a rout

under every door
light seeps like water,
a faint wash of peach,
then rising in a tidal surge,

light floods the east rooms
until the whole house
is lifted from the dark,
clarifying vague shapes

into a table's sharp edge,
a steepled candlestick,
paired patterned rugs,
and on her bed,

the pages of an open book
where printed paragraphs
leap from lines to letters
and one spot of sun

illuminates
a capital
O

SUNDAYS

Her drawer of "secrets"
comes back to me now:
Holy Cards, baseball cards,
one pair of tiny earrings,
mixed with lottery tickets --
relics shared with me on
Sundays with Nora.

At the Bronx flat she kept,
more home to me than home,
its red Castro convertible
its butter yellow curtains
its shamrocks in the kitchen
nothing matched
everything fit.

My parents left me there;
while they went visiting
we went to morning mass
at Our Lady of Refuge
and afternoon matinees
at the vast Loews Paradise
names ironic old iconic.

Passing then from the
church's clouds of incense
to the starlit clouds painted
on the ceiling of the theatre,
with its magic movie screen;
all of it blurring and blending
together into one miracle.

Afterwards we went to Krum's
for chocolate-mint sodas
and I'd feel an inner sinking
as the day drained away;
soon I must be returned
to my other world with its
silences and slamming doors.

Give me Sundays
without Mass
without movies
without mints
only this magic:
Peace

GREEN

We were snapping beans,
one yawning iron pot
between us where the
fresh pods smelled green.

Silent as statuary, we sat
knee to knee, bone to bone,
overlapping laps were one
in this kitchen's sanctuary.

Late afternoon's sepia light
pooled all around us
as the clock chimed four;
the day was fast passing.

At night I dreaded the dark
when I heard parental fights
and china smashed tonight;
I raced to the kitchen again.

You were hemming a dress;
your needle trailed pale thread
like an unraveled spider's web;
your thimble caught the light.

Wordless, we sat listening as
you stitched, I watched, and
down the hall voices rose;
for us, an ordinary evening.

As sleep's shawl covered me
(or was it yours?) I curled
unafraid now, in your bed,
and dreamed in green.

SCENT

It was always near you,
that small brown bottle,
old-fashioned in looks
like the flask of a tonic
or one secret swallow
of dirt-cheap whiskey.

The bottle's label revealed
it was Essence of Vanilla
from the grocery's shelf,
and concocted for baking.
You used it as cologne,
a drop on each wrist,

and this mingled with
the smell of cigarettes,
always *Lucky Strikes*,
like leather and lace
the two went together
blue smoke, pale vanilla.

Safety smells like that
for me, though your brand
of vanilla is now extinct;
I buy it as soap and scent
and I savored tobacco's
aroma long after I quit.

Your empty *Lucky* packs
held Bobby Pins and the
empty brown bottles held
Holy Water and there, in
the fifties, recycled, was
Essence of Nora Larkin.

SEARCH FOR THE START

Nora would say magic began it:
A chant against evil created our poems;
we try to outwit the dark with our words.

If we give voice to astute incantations,
recited, repeated, remembered, revered,
night cannot breathe on us as we sleep,

and as we wake, light will lean toward us,
as a mother bends over a crying child —
if we speak the right words the right way.

Whom do we summon with such mysteries?
Whose power is it we conjure and seek?
How do we learn what to say and not say?

It is ourselves and our own inner power
we hope to distill and decant into words;
If we say what we see, we see what we say.

DANCING

making a poem is dancing in place
so you told me
as we set our feet in the oven

that cavern's edge was our hearth
on wintry days
it was there you danced so often

if it was a jig or a reel or a waltz
you knew the steps
the beat sharpened and softened

set on "Low" the stove exhaled its
warming breath
on a child and a dancing woman

the light went from amber to cobalt
when you stopped
you'd drawn poetry from the oven

FOUND

Finally I found
where you began:
a quiet Irish county;
the village of Kilcree:

Sewn into the land,
a pocket of a place,
on a rich robe of earth;
too small for most maps.

Four snipped streets,
two thready lanes,
a church spire's needle
— a parish of 502 souls.

Clocks tick slower here,
attuned to the town's
pensive pulse and
tepid temperature.

All tans and browns;
dull as a blunt knife,
Kilcree could be, but
you also remembered

Hazy fields where cows
appeared to float at sea;
meadows of wild flowers
yellow-gold as cats' eyes.

Rock walls, stone on stone,
laid by hands gone to dust;
the rocks recall you at play
in blood-watered grasses.

I find your father's school
and house, empty now,
the whitewashed walls
faded, frail, enduring.

Here you first saw light,
here your life unfurled.
Here, too, within yours,
my own story lay curled.

NORA AT FORTY

Iwatch her as she beats the spuds
into submission with her muscular
right arm and her rough red hands;
nothing new about this daily ritual,

but I see eleven threads of silver,
by my count, in her flaming hair,
and a new crease in her forehead,
near that throbbing purple vein.

She would be forever young, so I
believed when I was small: Her skin
like risen cream, her ginger mane;
she was unchanged, always there,

untiring, long-striding, but now as
I look on I see the years of work
have cut a deep channel into her
and I watch as if to keep her here.

Raising me, perhaps, has aged her
or was it this troubled household?
What happens to others cannot,
must not will not happen to her,

more mother than mother, whose
food built my blood, whose words
filled my brain, whose grit saved
my life, whose faith is mine, she

cannot age or die and I will go
find the magic to make that so —
but first I will sit her down
and pummel those potatoes.

PEELING APPLES

You peeled apples
with a twist or two
of your deft wrist,
whenever you
incised the brittle
blood-red skin
of a Macintosh
into one thin
trailing curl.

Without a pause,
you carved spirals
of the fruited flesh,
shaving it layer by
layer, like a mesh,
as the apple's girth
swiftly diminished,
exposing the core
when you had
finished.

As a child, I watched
this ritual with awe
but I didn't grasp
then what I saw:
Time's action on life,
swift, subtle, silent
as a scalpel or a knife,
peeling years away,
layer after layer
day by day by day,
until we are honed
to the bone.

ANNIVERSARY FLOWERS

What can I leave at your grave that is new?
Only these, my words, and my mined memory.
I prize what I, the finder, found in you
nor have you died despite death's thievery.

Much of what I am is you, redefined:
Your words stay on my lips and in my brain;
your magical tales and beliefs are mine —
Superstitions, as well, complete my gains.

You cannot change or cease to be
but live on without myth or mystery.
At last I can claim you, flaming, in me
without hiding our entwined histories.

We survived common and uncommon strife.
Was it more than your spirit giving me life?

6
Remembering

WAITING

A watched pot never boils
unless you're boiling vodka

which I don't recommend
since flames escape flambés.

Fire: I fear it love it hate the
danger coiled within its gift

but this wild thing, tamed,
calls poetry from us

blended with past voices
with or without spirits

save the poet's and
the flickering listening light

something in a fire conjures
percolating pots of words,

those we watch gratefully
until the brew of magic roils.

STORED SECRETS

The closets whisper
as they do in houses
where there's been
a recent death.

I turn the door knobs,
resistant fists, guarding
all the secrets of this
troubled home.

In a bedroom closet
I find the hiding place
for my father's oldest
black medical bag.

Time lurches to a stop
like a balky train as
the bag spills its
hidden contents.

Left for me are letters,
love notes, confessions
— all I do not want
to see, to read, to know.

I could shut the bag,
forget this find and life
might go on as it was
and it might not.

When the train stops here
you get off or you go on
whatever you decide you
will always be different.

FOR MY FATHER

Lit, his bent head shines.
Balding now, he reads
as if he were only nine
when he would feed
on books of any kind.

Planted thick with words,
each page was a field
where he tramped unheard
through crops concealed,
dreaming, undisturbed.

In the crowded flat
above his mother's store
he read scientific tracts
and, thirsting for more,
he studied, swatting rats.

Now I watch him skim
his surgical tomes —
like Merlin he works
spells on flesh and bone;
wherever illness lurks.

I focus on his hands,
those of a musician,
playing on command:
a pensive physician
sifting mental sands.

In his study's nook I may
draw with colored pens.
From the arched doorway
his quick gaze descends
on the sketch I did today.

"Who's next?" He teases.
"God." I lower my eyes,
catching my blunder.
An ardent atheist, he sighs
but contains his thunder.

This man of science
sired an artistic mystic
(without his compliance),
but she'll outgrow that tic,
he thinks, it's mere defiance.

"How does this God look?"
My father is joking now.
"Like you, at a bookshelf--"
I break off, fearing a row,
and retreat into myself.

At six, I dread the future
but he relies on tact
to function as sutures;
I hide my doubts on that.
The prognosis? Inexact.

JOY

He, too, kissed a girl he never knew
on the borders of Times Square;
it seemed the only thing for him to do,
the war had ended, church bells rang,
everybody crowed and cried and sang.
New York twirled like a silver baton,
it slanted and it tilted and it lifted;
my father did not doubt the news
and he'd swear up and down for you
he somehow knew that it was true.
The girl he kissed was blue-eyed
with moist crimson lips, that's all
he can recall — he would not
wash her lipstick off his shirt and
kept it like a lady's dinner napkin
to remind him that day happened.

THE SURGEON

Asleep, he sees the body of his patient as a roadmap's duplication:
blue expressways and, in red, a shortcut to the beating destination.

Awake, he sees the faces of his patients as silk-screened originals,
an artist's expression, the pain of each unique and virginal.

At home, he cuts into filet mignon and sees a scalpel, not a knife.
"You're always too involved," snaps his attractive and acerbic wife.

"How should I be?" He impales asparagus on a fish fork's tines.
"Detached." Her brow lifts. "You haven't touched your wine."

"I will." Actually, he wants to check a patient in Progressive Care.
"You won't." Like an MRI she looks within. "You'll go back there."

"I can't talk to you about it, Claire." His neck has tightened.
His wife's voice, like her eyes, is glacial-green. "Forget it, then."

"I'll be quick." He rises from the table. "For dessert, I'm sure."
"Sure." Silent, she freezes into a sculpture of the late Liz Taylor.

Driving, he recalls his wife, nude, and pulls over, skimming grass.
Then he sees the roadmap of his patient's body and he hits the gas.

ELEGY FOR EVA

Bent into a hoop, you died,
your spine like a waning moon.
The housekeeper was horrified
to find you fading one May noon.

Before illness stole your teaching
you filled minds like wells with ink,
prodding, probing, not preaching,
you trained your novices to think.

You who cracked the eggshell
of the world open for me —
you, Circe, who knew well
where the yolk would be.

You were left inside the shell
of your own twisted bones;
during that last year of hell
you were too often alone.

Errand services, they say,
brought you food and wine,
new books from Doubleday,
and *The New York Times*.

You wanted nothing more;
privacy was your only need,
or so I was reassured —
I was too easily deceived.

You cherished select friends,
not only Woolf and Keats:
their presence, a Godsend,
and beloved symphonies.

This comforts me today:
your FM radio, a gift,
played as you slipped away;
Beethoven gave his Fifth.

CANTALOUPE

a tear on the tine of her fork
caught the light
and hung suspended
after she hid her face

from the noon buzz
of a café featuring
squid the day after
her father's funeral

she lowered her hand
the tear fell like old rain
from ancient eaves
though the pain was new

our desserts arrived
in the form of
brazen orange/pink
slabs of cantaloupe
seeming more salmon
than summer fruit

another tear
from her eyes
watered the melon
then more then more
and together we stared
as the cantaloupe
filled our vision

expanding ever-wider
until the melon offered
its heft and its length
as a welcome basin
for her for me
for all who have left
a tear on a tine

IN ATTENDANCE

I pass the tray of soaps and hand the towels out
and when the women leave I tidy up the sinks.
Sometimes a coin clangs in the fine china dish.

It's not a bad place work, all things considered:
the Ladies Room of a famous Manhattan hotel
where you tend to get a pretty refined clientele.

This is the only Ladies' Room I know about
that has wrapped soaps and orchids.
I gaze at the orchids when things get slow.

I always fear someone will remember me
from the grand apartment on Central Park
where I baked souffles and set formal tables.

I don't want them to know about my
change of fortune but that won't come to be.
No one in this room ever looks at me.

AT THE COUNTER

Hands, I know hands, they're my life,
I've sold women's gloves for thirty
years and I've seen it all, the soft
young hands sliding right into fine
buttery leather and the old arthritic
hands like mine that take tact and
a tug or two or three or four or
maybe more, and everything in
between because it's true, you
can tell a lot about people from
their hands, maybe more than
they might realize, like the ones
with bitten nails and those with
"Writer's Bump" on the second
finger and then there are those
touchy, upscale hands with
their impeccable manicures,
be careful with that type, you
must be reverential to their
owners but they always buy
the big ticket items, bet on it,
and now you get the girls with
green and purple fingernails,
but you don't comment, you
sell them reds and leopard
prints and say, "Have a nice
day," in the end it's worth it,
somehow it has to be,
hands, yes I know hands.

THE BLIND PIANO TUNER

In his darkness he sees keys:
tongues of ivory and onyx
eighty-eight in orderly array
one of life's few constancies

Like a doctor making calls
he visits each piano *in situ*:
parlors, foyers, niches and,
with pride, Carnegie Hall.

He knows all their voices,
none the same. His tuning
fork makes each diagnosis;
cures require apt choices.

By touch, by ear, he tightens
strings, replaces hammers,
and whenever the true pitch
sounds his darkness lightens.

Too many pianos sit alone,
untouched, ornamental, and
he dares to play them, just a
bit, when no one is at home.

On his second-hand upright,
he concertizes on his own.
Favoring Rachmaninoff, he
plays often late into the night.

He dreams in color even now:
flying red pianos fill a purple
sky, high above yellow grass
and sometimes an azure cow.

"Don't presume to pity me,"
he screams inwardly at
sighted people. "I hear
more than you can see."

PROTEST

"Take your hands off me — desist!"
I want to shout. "Who permitted
you to pound my keys this way,
even if you're trying to play Liszt?"

I have a voice, there is no doubt,
but I speak notes and scores, not
words, and therein lies frustration:
I can't stop the touch of a lout.

Don't think of me as an elitist,
though I *am* a Steinway. I delight
in music, well-rendered, but I fear
I may become a defeatist.

What to do when children fix
their eyes on me, "their toy"
and two of them bang out that
piece called, "Chopsticks?"

My owners ignore me, sad to say,
except for holidays and parties.
I may scream if I am forced
again into a "Happy Birthday."

Now and then a guest takes time
to play, with a respectful touch,
Gershwin or some Chopin or
Rachmaninoff — sublime!

One man comes with regularity
and shivers my strings with his
rendition of "Stravinsky."
I look forward to his singularity.

He is my tuner, a blind man,
whose deft touch is intimate
— he alone caresses me.
I await the feel of his hand.

SUMMER MORNING

I remember how my eyes
fluttered open on his face
one early summer morning

in a room filling with light
as he smoothed the sheets
across my sleeping sprawl.

Into the layered lake of life
that instant sank away, I
thought, but still it surfaces,

and with it surface other
random instants like glass
shards washing ashore

from my childhood's dawns:
the bluest of milk pitchers
and a sunlit silver spoon and

above the lake, merged with
wind, comes a silky sound:
the rustlings of an oak and

a tree tapping on the roof
above the bed where my eyes
fluttered open on his face

THE ATTIC

After all this time she
still surrenders to that
shy August afternoon
its light like lemonade
spilling into her small
attic of a workroom
with its simple sounds:
a sighing closet door
that creaking rocker
six bunched daisies
whispering in a faint
breath of breeze
the expectant desk
and listening books
under ancient eaves
a tentative tap of the
red maple's branch
against the window
and the tap of keys
on an old typewriter
the room's pulse
drawing from the air
strands of linked words
from God knows where

IF WALLS TALKED

Certainly our houses know us
better than we know ourselves
they recognize each footstep

voice whisper shout creak of
stairs squawk of springs who
slams who swears who sings

but a house knows still more
of deeply imprinted regrets
rejoicing and recriminations

the walls, though mute, talk
in ways we sense if we let
borders reveal atmospheres

waiting there for years
so if you settle into silence
a house draws around you

and you feel cobalt despair
sterling calm and red's edges
from mercy to mirth to malice

imprints on a house remain
indelible as they mingle with
the layers others left here

in the paint the plastering
imbedded in the floorboards
unknown to realtors' agents

DYNAMICS

FRIEND
A rock-bound jetty reaching into changing seas,
wide enough for two laughing striding easily

Hand grips hand as curling waves drench stone;
hazed by spray the jetty upholds its own.

ENEMY
A sharpened arrowhead, resistant to weather,
aging, guilt; proud as a war-bonnet's feather.

It may wait for years, poisoned, on the shelf,
but withheld, an arrowhead turns against itself.

MARRIAGE
A book's facing pages with one line between them
defying its spine the binding is freedom.

ELEMENTS
Once I felt the flaming dart of malice.
Once I felt a grudge's hefty weight.

Often I have felt mercy's solace
and its quiet release we all await.

Hate and malice only go so far.
Mercy's powers daze the stars.

DEMONS

there are people I don't want to see again
not now not ever not even in the afterlife;
why then do they invade my dreams,
at times, against a field of poison green?

why must I gaze, with eerie clarity,
at that freckled kid who led his peers
to chant, "creep creep creep" at me?
I recall his taunting face, his tidy name.

why view that later traitor surfacing like
a great white shark, plunging through my
sleep's seas after twenty-five long years?
I hoped she had vanished in time's winds.

I prefer my dreams of massy summer trees,
and on their branches each leaf bears a
face, alive and luminous and laughing,
twittering like larks, "Remember me?"

Time to call that exorcist, in high demand,
whose specialty is ghosts, living or dead,
and let him perform his mental surgery
if he can work me into his busy ministry.

WEATHER

it is a vortex
it is a funnel
it is a cyclone
it is home

this home has weather swings:
a Manhattan penthouse —
apparently staid and serene —
is a tornado packing winds
of three hundred miles an hour

by day, silver on the sideboard
aged brandy in the library
chiming crystal chandeliers:
subtle but significant signs,
seen by appointment only

by night, with few witnesses,
silver is a missile to be hurled
lamps crash, brandy cascades,
shards of a wine glass glint —
the tornado has touched down

every evening the child hovers
outside the master bedroom
where she waits for the voices
to rise and finally it begins:
the twister, the parental fight

his voice rumbles like a truck
in the street while the other is
cool steel, a straight razor
cleaving the room's taut air,
scented with jasmine and gin

the fighters, practiced, throw
words like sharpened knives
aimed precisely to draw blood
— louder now; the child bolts
for the kitchen's protection

tonight she snatches the
hall's photo of her parents
years before and, weary of
fear, angry at pain, she
smashes the photo's frame.

THE GRANDMOTHERS

I said it was no good
my son smart-as-a whip
the big time surgeon
with that woman,
that what,
that debutante?

Did she know what's it's like to be poor?
my boy worked his way through school
and she got it all handed to her?
I don't care if she's pretty,
looks like Liz Taylor, they say?

Well, she's a snob and snobs
are not pretty but that's how
she got her claws in my son.
This is the first stupid thing he's done.
I can just hear her mother.

~~

I said from the start this was a mistake
A disaster, actually, how could it thrive?
My daughter, cultured, cultivated,
an Ivy League graduate, with her
breeding, her background —

with that man, the son of a Gypsy and a
half-Jewish peddler growing up in a slum?
What kind of mix could that make?
I don't care if he's a rising young surgeon,
I don't care if he's brilliant as Edison.

There are other surgeons but she wanted
this one, the star of the moment, and
the child, what of the child?

PEONIES IN JERSEY

I never called her "Mother."
She disapproved of "Mom."
We were never close —
distance was our only bond.

She is ash now.
This, her final wish;
and I obey directions:
Private. Bury ashes.
Do not scatter from
some tacky ferry.
A crematorium is
requested, "even
though the place
is in New Jersey."

An urn? Perhaps a
decorative box for
the "cremains?"
The funeral director
asks. "Cremains?"
she would have said,
with that arched brow,
eyeing the man's
frankly yellow tie.
"We'll take good care
of her," he promises.
"Leave it all to me."

I will. I have. I do.
And now I kneel
on the grass of a
"Memorial Garden,"
as directed, and
as stated, in the
state of New Jersey.
There is an abstract
slate fountain and
a pruned rose garden.

I'm staring down a
small oblong shaft
in the spaded earth.
Beside me is a man
with a dark liquid
gaze, maybe seventy.

He holds a silver box.
I give the gravedigger
a Phi Beta Kappa key.
He lays this on the lid
of the canister, then
gives the box to me.

I hold it for a minute
and I think of her
nail polish, *Cherries*
in the Snow, the
elegant forehead,
that knowing glance.
The click of silken
slippers in the hall.

I set the box into the
earth. Is it heavier
for an only child like
me? Still kneeling,
I say the prayers she
didn't want, I need.

We brought flowers,
white peonies, too
lush, too many for
this elfin grave. I
leave one. When I
stand, my eyes are
dry and my knees
are wet and green.

As we leave, I
turn to watch the
gravedigger lift
his spade to
smooth the earth.
I think of her as
ash, buried as she
wished, with her
small bronze key.

We take the eleven
peonies away and
scatter them into
the churning wake
of the next Staten
Island Ferry.

White water, white spray.
Petals white as bone.

NOTES ON THE AUTHOR

Marcy Heidish is an award-winning author of twelve books, fiction and non-fiction. Her first novel, *A WOMAN CALLED MOSES*, was made into a television movie starring Cicely Tyson.

Ms. Heidish has written numerous published short pieces and also poetry for thirty years.

She is the recipient of a National Endowment for the Arts Creative Writing Fellowship Grant, a L.I.N.K.S. Award, a Schubert Fellowship, a finalist for an "Edgar" Award, and other honors.

Ms. Heidish has taught at Georgetown University, The George Washington University, Howard University, and Fordham University. She has conducted numerous writing workshops and seminars.

In addition, Ms. Heidish has been a long-term volunteer in shelters for homeless women, a volunteer on a metropolitan hotline, a hospice, and the Lighthouse for the Blind.

Born in New York City and a long-time resident of Washington, D.C., Marcy Heidish now lives and writes in the American southwest.

Marcy Heidish
Sample of Published Works

Critical Acclaim For Novels By Marcy Heidish

A WOMAN CALLED MOSES

-Award-winning, best-selling novel based on the life of Harriet Tubman, abolitionist and conductor on the Underground Railroad.
-A Literary Guild Alternate Selection;
-A Bantam paperback.
-A TV Movie, starring Cicely Tyson, still available on DVD.
- Houghton Mifflin Co., 1st Publisher

Praise for *A Woman Called Moses*:

• **Publishers Weekly**: "Her story has been told before, but never as eloquently, almost poetically, as here...achingly real...a strong narrative of a totally committed woman, one who speaks directly to our own desperate need to feel committed — and our wish that somewhere in the world there were more people like Harriet Tubman."

• **Washington Post Book World**: "Profoundly rewarding ...a daring work of the imagination."

• **Chicago Sun Times**: "Marcy Heidish has, almost un-cannily, crawled into the skin and very mind of Harriet Tubman.... The dialogue sings with poetic beauty."

• **Houghton Mifflin Co.**: "As events build toward a stunning climax on the Underground Railroad, we are drawn into the spellbinding narrative of an extraordinary life, and a portion of our American past."

WITNESSES

- Award-winning novel based on the life of lay minister Anne Hutchinson, America's first female advocate of religious freedom.
- Citation: Society for Colonial Wars; laudatory reviews; large-print edition published as well as hardcover and paperback versions.
- Houghton Mifflin Co., 1st Publisher

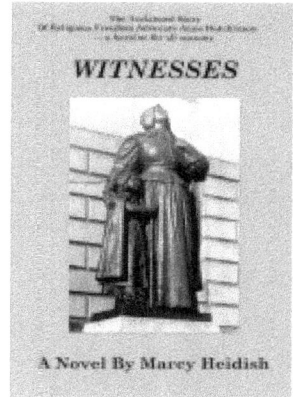

Praise for *Witnesses:*

- *The New York Times Book Review*: " ...nothing ordinary about her creation of this remarkable woman. The novel abounds in literary grace. It employs the voices of the times as though heard this minute."

- *The New Yorker Magazine*: "A striking novel...a compelling portrait."

- *The Washington Post*: "Pure pleasure. Anne Hutchinson is real; thanks to *Witnesses,* she at last assumes her proper place...in American history." —Jonathan Yardley, Pulitzer Prize-winning critic.

- *Ballantine Books*: "This fearless woman, mother of fifteen, a leader in medicine and politics, comes to vivid life in these pages. A true believe in religious freedom who paid dearly for her principles in two trials for heresy. In the tradition of Arthur Miller's *The Crucible*, Witnesses is the deeply felt portrait of a woman in the paranoid climate of 17th century Boston."

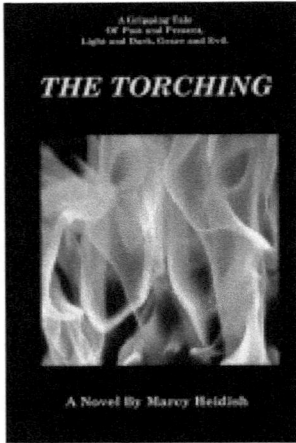

THE TORCHING

-Acclaimed contemporary novel, in hardcover and paperback.
- Literary Guild Alternate Selec-tion; laudatory reviews.
- Optioned for TV movie.
- Simon & Schuster, 1st Publisher.

Praise for *The Torching*:
- ***Washington Post Book World***: "Because of Heidish's skill, we get the full force of her double-wham-my...in part due to the grace with which she weaves the present-day and the historical, but also because of her inventiveness at the book's close, the daring way she gets both strands of plot to unite.... Marcy Heidish is a stylish and intelligent novelist to boot, more than up to the dizzy-ing, tale-spinning task that she set for herself here."
- ***Kirkus Reviews:*** "Shuddery mystery-suspense with super-natural overtones."
- ***Library Journal:*** "Intricately constructed...A deliciously spine-tingling, multi-layered literary mystery..."
- ***Publishers Weekly***: "Subtle and gratifying psychological suspense...Penetrating characterizations...Heidish im-peccably orchestrates the historical and contemporary, the super-natural and psychological."
- ***Baltimore Sun:*** "Fine, goose-pimply."
- ***Denver Post:*** "Macabre ride...Eerie...Intriguing... Frigh-tening surprises...Enjoy."
- ***Arizona Daily Star***: "An imaginative, amazing writer... A magician with words."
- ***New York Daily News***: "Compellingly readable and likely to induce the screaming-meemies."

THE SECRET ANNIE OAKLEY

- Acclaimed novel based on the life of the legendary sharp-shooter.
- In addition to hard- and paperback versions, a *Readers Digest* Condensed Novel.
- Optioned for film.
- Translated into several languages, laudatory reviews.
- New American Library, 1st Publisher.

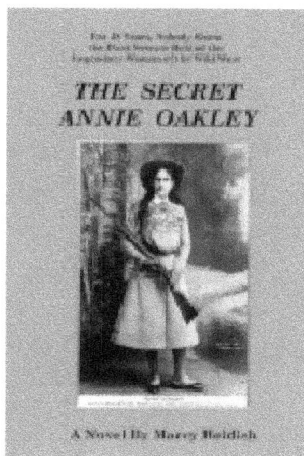

Praise for *The Secret Annie Oakley:*

- **Kirkus Reviews**: "An immensely touching and cohesive fictional biography of the legendary sharp-shooter... builds from exemplary research to a fresh portrait of a talented woman in crisis...a class act—as Heidish reconstructs. with color and drama, the choreography of the shows, the tone of the period, and the textures of a haunting past."

- **The Arizona Daily Star**: "... an imaginative, amazing writer ... a magician with words.... Each character has been brought to life with a mere pen stroke; flesh and blood beings that are more than fiction.... A masterpiece of creative writing."

- **The Kansas City Star**: "An unforgettable story."

MIRACLES

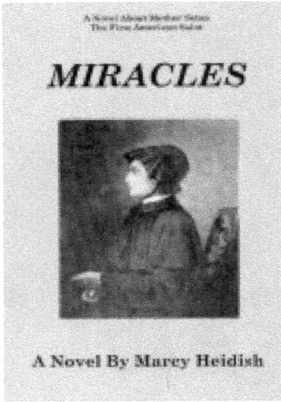

MIRACLES

A Novel By Marcy Heidish

- Historical novel based on the life of **Mother Elizabeth Seton**, first American-born canonized saint.
- Main selection, *The Catholic Book Club*.
- New American Library, 1st Publisher.

Praise for *Miracles*:

• *New American Library*: "*Miracles* is the story of an unforgettable woman's life and love. It is a novel charged with the vitality of a life that saw many changes, and with the power of a love that took many forms ... [whether] as a lonely daughter of a wealthy, indifferent man; a searching young woman; a contented matron embracing a marriage that produced five beloved children; a widow searching for new meaning to life."

• *The New York Times Book Review*: "This appealing book, told from the point of view of a skeptical modern priest, moves swiftly through tragedy to triumph."

• *Kirkus Reviews:* "Working delicately with a balance of Church hagiography and psychological insight, Ms. Heidish provides another strong focus on the root dilemma of female saints and achievers."

DEADLINE

-Contemporary psychological novel with a "mystery" as a narrative line.
-Nominee for prestigious national "Edgar" Award; fine reviews.
- St. Martin's Press, 1st Publisher.

Praise for *Deadline*:

• **Washington Post**: *"Deadline* is a tense, well-turned tale, filled with authentic police and newspaper people. Heidish's taut, punchy style moves the story at lightning speed."

• **Kirkus Reviews**: "The high-tension plot is enhanced by sharply etched pictures, by many vivid characters, and by a crisp, clean, first-person style. Heidish imbues her haunting story and her gutsy heroine with a rare sense of tenderness and poignancy. An impressive mystery by a gifted writer."

• **St. Martin's Press**: "This wire-tight novel probes re-lentlessly, driving deep into psychological darkness and violent death. As the riveting story reaches its stunn-ing conclusion, we see a complex woman forced to meet the ultimate deadline."

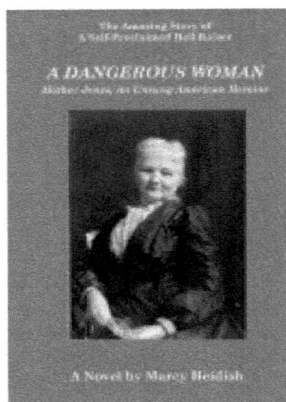

A Dangerous Woman: Mother Jones, An Unsung American Heroine

- A compelling, inspiring new historical novel, another powerful "profile in courage" American-style novel based on the life of Mary Harris Jones, a self-proclaimed Hell Raiser, daring labor leader and colorful, quirky humanitarian

• The arresting novel of an indomitable force, dressed demurely in widow's weeds and lace collars who:
• As an Irish immigrant – lost her homeland to the Great Famine.
• As a wife and mother – lost her whole family to yellow fever.
• As a dressmaker – lost home and business to the Chicago Fire
• As a survivor – turned from sorrow to help others survive.

Follow one of America's most feisty, fearless...and forgotten heroines whose rallying cry was:

"PRAY FOR THE DEAD — AND FIGHT LIKE HELL FOR THE LIVING!"

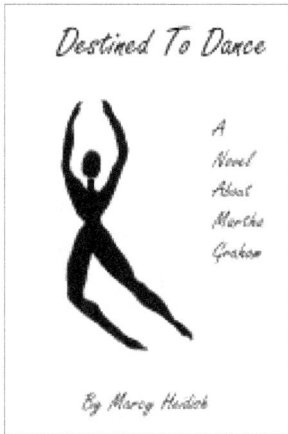

DESTINED TO DANCE
A Novel About Martha Graham

They called her a genius.
They called her a goddess.
They called her a monster.

Which title best fits Martha Graham, iconic Mother of Modern Dance?

Find out — in the <u>first historical novel</u> about this great American diva.

DESTINED TO DANCE is a creative portrait of the legendary dancer and choreographer. Heidish offers another remarkable account of an American heroine: her successes, her sorrows, and her struggles.

Here is a masterful portrait of Graham, on stage, back-stage, offstage. We see Graham's break-through brilliance, often compared to Picasso's or Sravinsky.

We also witness Graham's triumph over alcoholism, despair, and a failed marriage. Set against the intriguing world of dance, Martha Graham's story offers us a close-up on a complex and compelling overcomer.

Martha Graham (1894-1991) invented a new "language of movement," still taught around the world and exemplified in such classic works as *Appalachian Spring*, among 180 others.

As always, Heidish's research is thorough and her sense of her subject is magical.

For all who love the arts, all who seek inspiration, and all who like to read between history's lines, ***DESTINED TO DANCE*** is a must-read book.

NON-FICTION BOOKS:

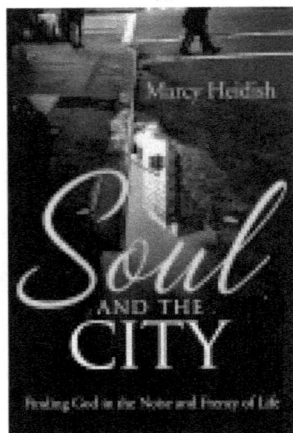

■ *Soul and the City*, WaterBrook Press, Random House imprint

Praise for *Soul and the City*:

• Rick Hamlin, executive editor of *Guideposts* and author of *Finding God on the A Train*: "I actually started reading Marcy Heidish's *Soul and the City* on a subway train, and I must say it had exactly the effect she writes about. It gave me peace in the middle of the hurry, the rush, the loud noise of the city."

• Leigh McLeroy, author of *The Beautiful Ache* and *The Sacred Ordinary*: "... a rich and nuanced touring companion to rival any Michelin or Eyewitness guide—usable in any city of the world. Keep it close and...you will meet beauty and holiness no matter where you pause to look."

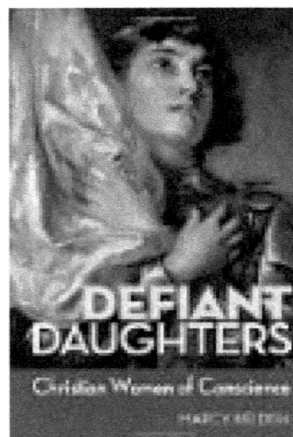

● ● ● ●

■ *Defiant Daughters*, Liguori Publications.

Praise for *Defiant Daughters*:

• *Liguori Publications*: Joan of Arc, Immaculée Ilibagiza, Corrie ten Boom, and Sojourner Truth are among those women whom best-selling author Marcy Heidish calls "Defiant Daughters."

Inspiring and compelling stories of courageous women whose strength was fed by their spirituality. Heidish seeks out the decisive juncture where each took a stand for conscience, however high the cost.

What motivated these "defiant daughters," who gave their all for God? Heidish seeks out the decisive juncture where they took a stand for conscience, regardless of the consequences. This stunning and compelling book will bring you face-to-face with an unforgettable female gallery of "profiles in courage."

••••

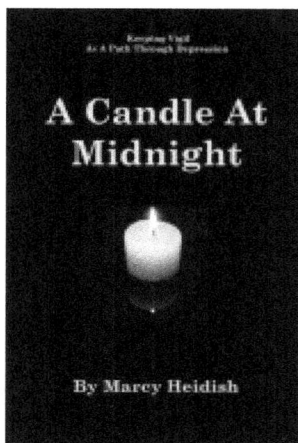

■ *A Candle At Midnight*, Ave Maria Press.

<u>Prase for *A Candle At Midnight*</u>:
• Alen J. Salerian, M.D., Medical Director of the Washington Psychiatric Center: "Heidish honors modern medicine and spiritual healing in this compelling work."

• Martha Manning, Author of *Undercurrents: A Life Beneath the Surface*: "This is not a book of abstractions.... I recommend this book to anyone who is caught in the darkness of mid-night."

• Rev. Nancy Eggert, Spiritual Director: "A masterpiece!"

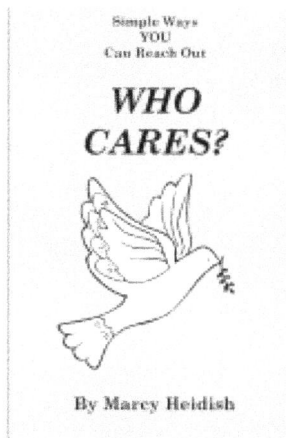

••••

■ *Who Cares? Simple Ways YOU Can Reach Out*, Ave Maria Press.

<u>Praise for *Who Cares?*</u>:
• *Ave Maria Press*: A lonely neighbor, a colleague in distress, a friend in difficulty. In situations like these we want to reach out and help, yet so often we feel unsure about our response. What to do? What to say? What is enough? Too much? Too little?

This practical book is designed to bring out the caring person in each of us. Marcy Heidish offers simple, specific ways to practice the art of caring, especially within our immediate circle of concern: family, friends, neighbors, and coworkers.... Heidish reminds us of the many little things we can do to open the door to a caring relationship.

• *Cultural Information Service*: "Contains savvy insights and wisdom about service... This is an ideal resource for anyone interested in engaged spirituality."

Short Pieces:

- Articles and book reviews published in *Ms.* Magazine, *GEO* Magazine, *The Washington Post, The Washington Star*, and various in-flight periodicals. Two of these pieces are:
  - "The Pilgrim Who Stayed," *GEO* Magazine, about Chartres Cathedral, widely translated.

  - "The Grand Dame of the Harbor," about the Statue of Liberty, was a highly acclaimed cover story for *GEO* Magazine. This article is included in a textbook anthology designed to teach writing to college students. Winner of coveted Apex Award.

See Marcy Heidish page at
www.Amazon.com [AND Kindle] *

* Marcy Heidish Books are distributed by Ingram of Ingram Content Group Inc., the world's largest distributor of physical and digital content, providing books, music and media content to over 38,000 retailers, libraries, schools and distribution partners in 195 countries. More than 25,000 publishers use Ingram's ....